"It is a poet's job to tell the truth. Ray McNiece strips away the multiple coats of yellowing varnish in *Our Way of Life* laying bare a distressed yet solidly built realism. Rather than the usual pop cynicism—these poems embrace an idealism of what should and could be while invoking the language of a poet's poet. Like a canary in a coal mine he beckons us to come above ground and breathe deep—before it is too late."

—Michael Salinger, ClevelandPoetics, author of *Neon*

"Ray McNiece's poetry comes to us just in time as a voice that recognizes the political dissatisfaction of an America stuck in a war that there seems to be no words for. He exposes "flag draped coffins/they won't let us see" as he criticizes the Bush administration's call for war in "Who Killed America?" McNiece's poetic conversations on America journey from the White House lawn to the banks of Ohio's Chagrin River, where the poet explores his own connections to America in the best poem of this collection, "Love Song for Cleveland," a poem that seems destined to be set to music. In this timely collection, McNiece provides answers to important questions many Americans fail to ask during our troubled times.*Our Way of Life* recognizes the void where language meets protest through poetry."

—Claire McMahon

Other Books by Ray McNiece

The Bone Orchard Conga (Wordsmith Press)

The Road that Carried Me Here (Bottom Dog Press)

Song that Fathoms Home (Bottom Dog Press)

Wet Sand, Raven Tracks (deep cleveland press)

Dis—Voices From a Shelter (Fractal Edge)

Us? Talking Across America (Fractal Edge)

America Zen, Co-Edited with Larry Smith, (Bottom Dog Press)

Music/Poetry CDs by Ray McNiece

The Road that Carried Me Here (Wordsmith)

Mouth Music (Flip City Records)

Love Song for Cleveland (Page to Stage Music)

BOTTOM DOG PRESS

Our Way of Life

Poems

Ray McNiece

11/1/13

Working Lives Series
Bottom Dog Press
Huron, Ohio

ISBN 978-1-933964-14-0

Bottom Dog Press
PO 425/ Huron, OH 44839
http://members.aol.com/Lsmithdog/bottomdog

Photographic Art
by Anita Herzog and Ray McNiece

These poems appeared originally in the following Journals, Books, and E-Zines:
"And the Jazz Plays On," "Who Killed America" and "Love Song for Cleveland" in *Whiskey Island*. "Love Song for Cleveland" was subsequently reprinted in *The Cleveland Reader.* "Our Way of Life," "Atomic Milk" and "Mike Salinger Explodes Time" in *Moonlit*. "Rat's Teeth" in *Art Crimes, Volume 25*. "Grunt" and "Attack of the Giant Cockroaches" were published in different versions in *Us? Talking Across America,* Fractal Edge Press 2004. "Tanks Are Rolling" appeared in the e-zine *November3rd Club*.

Ray McNiece can be reached at this homepage:
http://www.raymcniece.com

Table of Contents

I. *Our Way of Life*

II. *Blue Sky Beyond*

Our Way of Life

Flag Coffins

Woke up dead today,
tethered to my body
like a flag in the wind,
tugging from heart root
as it unknots, on hot
breeze of dying sky,
red dust in the east
from Fallujah's homes,
blown to America.

I went to the park
and read names carved
on war monuments,
boys once, their fathers
took them to ballgames,
all summer they played
war in the woods till
mom called them home,
flag draped coffins
they won't let us see.

Life During Wartime

No sparrows clamor the eaves,
no bawds of euphony chorus aurora.
Just the greasy chirp and gurgle of starlings,
remnants of what birds return in spring anymore,
and the window filling with another gray
Cleveland dawn, and rush hour news
on the radio as I hold her dreaming in my arms.

My own guts bloat from last night's 40 ounces
of cheap pain killer. I came to bed with the end
of the world on TV in my head and it hasn't gotten better.
The traffic copter over the freeway reports
congestion in the ozone haze ½ mile from here.
One junked theory demised the dinosaurs
by suffocation from methane gas percolating
from mountains of their own waste.
Whole forests collapsed, choked off,
that we use now to fuel our own autogeddon.

Or maybe I'm misremembering, cold mammal,
it was a scorching comet direct hit that did them in,
this little ball got too hot, or too cold
and their balls shrunk up, or they ate their own.
How the hell do I know, I wasn't there.
I'm here in bed with my love at the end
of the American dream, and in Babylon
they wait in line to fill up their tanks
right above the second largest oil reserve
in this desertified world, with imported gas,
as we feed our own addiction to fossil fuels.

Meanwhile GIs hand out 5s, 10s, and 20s,
from suitcases to survivors, as the euro rises,
and we pay another billion in hotel tabs
for mercenaries in the green zone,
while summer literacy camps close

from lack of funding so you can't read
all about, let alone read between the lines
since no one bothers to report
the roof of another school caving in.
You can hear Rome falling from here
as the traffic copter reports more jams.

Giant Energy Corporation scams no longer
make the lead story on the news.
Corporate media parrots the mantra
Let the market decide, as if it's God's word.
The politicians used to do what they did
when they thought no one was looking.
Now they do it out in the open
and under a huge flag, giving out $200
tax breaks in one hand, and picking 2 grand
out of back pockets with the other.
But I have get up to go to work and hope
I don't get as sick as those starlings gurgling
outside my window sound today.

Our Way Of Life

> *"The President will not sign any treaty that threatens our way of life."*
> *—Bush's press secretary on signing the Kyoto Accord*

No, we're not in Kansas anymore, Toto.
we lost our innocence long before the towers fell
in a swirl of world debt and desiccated sky,
our slow-mo disaster movie coming home to roost.

Every shred of Dorothy's red, white, and blue dress
got sucked up with the last family farm
in a swirl of White House spin control,
leaving Lady Liberty naked to the world.

But never mind that man behind the curtain
pulling the levers, *I am the great and powerful Oz!*
bellowing oil derrick flames and belching black smoke
covering the yellow brick road once paved with gold,

as America crumbles around us like a strip mall,
as the new mall shines somewhere over the rainbow,
off the next exit if only we pursue our happiness—
there's duct tape and plastic to keep out any ill wind.

Here come the flying monkeys, not Darwin's dupes,
but the winged troglodytes of the Kansas school board,
bibles disguised as science books in their paws,
proclaiming into law T*he earth was created flat.*

Back home the farm has become a McMansion,
Junior practices blowing up whatever flies towards him,
trying to take away his way of life—even Peter Pan
can't think good thoughts to save those lost boys now,

as the boys in the hood, the hicks from the sticks
and the *pachucos en el barrio* stay stuck in the desert

protecting our way of life in faulty Kevlar vests
rolling frankensteined humvees down some kids' street.

Stick a yellow ribbon on the back of those hummers
the suburban munchkins roll in, blasting gansta rap
through gated condos on their way to college,
fueled by dividends from Daddy Warbucks' Company,

while Dorothy lays in her room watching reality
shows and trying on poses of her favorite celebrities,
and dad stays drunk downstairs tuned into the big game
on big screen HDTV as mom drives out to get malled.

So nobody notices that bloated elephant
dying in the middle of the living room, tuskless,
big as an empty tanker truck, it's side tagged
with big red graffiti, *Our Way of Life.*

Who Killed America

There's a flag flying over my home town,
a flag flying over the library,
and a flag hanging over the cemetery
        at half mast and upside down,
        draped over two coffins coming home.
Who killed America just when we were all almost free?
Who killed our country? I sing of thee.
Not us, we were watching our big screen TVs.
Not us, we were driving our SUVs
to the mall on another shopping spree.
Who killed America? I sing of thee.

There's a man stressing down the street with clenched fists,
a woman limping from an alley who's never been kissed,
and a grey Uncle Sam vet in his VA bed,
        ill fed and shivering with dread—
        he'd be better off dead, the taxpayers said.
Who killed America just when we were all almost free?
Who killed our country? I sing of thee.
Not me, says the dealer, we have the cure,
if they can pay for the care.
Who said this world would be fair?
Who Killed America? I sing of thee.

There's a woman dancing naked to pay off her debts,
a workingman watching till his paycheck is spent;
and a thug knocking someone's grandma down
        as everyone else just stands around,
        not making a sound when she hits the ground.
Who killed America just when we were all almost free?
Who killed our country? I sing of thee.
Not me, says stripper, I'm trying to survive.
Not me, says the worker, all I do is strive
to stay alive and have some fun besides.
Who killed America? I sing of thee.

There's a husband cruising teens on his way to the burbs,
his trophy wife slumming those after-hours clubs,
a son playing games where he murders and robs,
        capping bodies into cartoon screams
        pixilated blood burning into his dreams.
Who killed America just when we were all almost free?
Who killed our country? I sing of thee
Not me, says the Adman, look at all you can buy.
Not me, says the buyer, why ask why?
I just want mine before I die.
Who killed America? I sing of thee.

There's a preacher proclaiming his kingdom has come,
klansmen burning crosses on someone's lawn,
and a teacher testing standards, ignoring the war,
        reciting names and dates and numbers,
        but never telling what we're dying for?
Who killed America just when we were all almost free?
Who killed our country? I sing of thee.
Not me, says the preacher, I'm God's chosen.
Not me, says the teacher, I'm not the one
who gave those lost children all their guns.
Who killed America? I sing of thee.

There's a newsman hiding blood behind his smile,
a demagogue who knows fear will sell,
and a commander in chief doing god's will,
        sending crusaders to guard his oil wells,
        never showing how their blood is spilled.
Who killed America just when we were all almost free?
Who killed our country? I sing of thee.
Not me, says the pundit, I'm always right
Not me, says the prez, God can't be wrong.
Not me, says the veep, who's pulling the strings.
Who killed America? I sing of thee.

There's a crack baby bawling in a charity ward crib,
a chick looking for rocks on the wrong side of town

  and a mother wailing over her blown-up son,
        the only job he got was carrying a gun,
        dying again for the rich man's gain.
Who killed America just when we were all almost free?
Who killed our country? I sing of thee.
Not me, says the child, I have no words.
Not me, says the mother, my boy is dead—
I already said, my boy is dead.
Who killed America? I sing of thee.

Tanks Are Rolling

Tanks are rolling on Baghdad,
speeding over miles and miles of scorched sand,
burning gallon upon gallon of overpriced oil,
chasing down Saddam's American funded army.

Tanks are rolling right past invisible weapons of mass distraction,
tearing across the UN Charter, the US Constitution,
and leaving Tom Paine's Common Sense in the dust.
Tanks are flattening the watchdog press,
corporate media stars along for the ride,
racing to guard the oil ministry
while looters steal the Babylonian Tablets
and torch the archives of civilization.

Tanks are rolling down the same highway of death
from the first Gulf War, charcoaled ghosts grinning from
        the berm
rolling down highway 49, that stretches all the way back
to Halliburtan's loading dock
where stacks of shells encased in uranium
wait to glow the sands like the plastic Jesus stuck
riding shotgun on a contract trucker's dashboard.

Tanks are rolling off assembly lines across America.
They may as well be rolling down the same road
in Florida where lines of blacklisted voters
were turned away from the polls,
or rolling through Midwestern drive-thrus
where consumers buy the burger deal—
a quarter pound of steroid-laced, anti-biotic resistant meat
that only cost one hundred gallons of fresh water,
two quarts of gas, three pounds of grain and one pound of topsoil
that took five hundred years to form as prairie
no longer even there anymore,
covered now with miles of feedlots, and acres of corn

leaching the earth as far as the eye cannot see
buffalo herds once grazing sweet grass.

Tanks are rolling ignorant that civilization depends upon
six inches of topsoil and the fact that it rains.
Tanks are rolling down the same access road
that opened the national parks to timber and mineral plunder
via a legal loophole big enough
to drive a Hummer's six thousand pounds of gross weight,
tax write-off luxury you deserve
right on through—try driving that through the eye of a needle!

The same Hummer the consumer drives
down the Ronald Reagun freeway
to the strip mall before the dollar store closes
so he can buy two new plastic flags
pressed by sweat shop workers in China
(where no man stands in front of a Tank in Tiananmen Square
anymore)
so he can fly them from both sides of that Hummer
just to let the boys at the front know
they are dying for fourteen miles per gallon,
the boys at the front scavenging junk piles for armor
to Frankenstein their own Humvees lumbering down
Baghdad's Boulevard of Improvised Explosive Devices.

But there is no stopping this son of God
Bless the U.S.A in his hurry to get home,
so don't get in his way or he'll blow you away
like they do in the Desert Storm Video Game.
He's got to get back to his gated community condo
at Eagle Creek (no eagle, no creek)
where he'll lock all the doors and settle in
to watch the last episode of Survivor.

Tanks are not rolling down the road map to peace,
They're staying the course for more war
to preserve our way of life,

rolling towards the final carnage of Autogeddon
fought in the sand over the black blood beneath
to decide once and for all
just whose God of which chosen people
can drop the bigger, better and stronger God Bomb –
Jaweh's mushroom cloud engulfing the whole world.

Zionist tanks, Jihad tanks, and Evangelical tanks
are all holy rolling down that same dead end
where a poets of Israel, the poets of Palestine,
the poets of Iraq, the poets of Iran,
and the poets of America make their stand
waving the white flags
of their poems.

No Child Left Behind

A shot of "no child left behind"
from an in-bedded photographer,
one of our boys cradling in his arms
an Iraqi boy amid the rubble
like a dusty, camouflaged pieta—
but no photo of his mother
blown apart by a smart bomb.
Network standards refuse her face.

If a child falls in the middle
of a bombed out foreign city
and there's no media around,
does it still make a sound?
Eyes have lids that can close,
every body's head can turn away
and mouths can always stay shut,
but the ears have no doors.

So what would Jesus not do?
Not U.S. Jesus of the missiles
dropping tons of bunker busters
to show the efficacy of pacification,
the blessing of his footfalls
towering clouds to heaven
leaving glowing tracks in the sand
through the cradle of civilization.

But this child of God born naked
of armor into this war, wandering
dazed from his blasted home
who stumbles onto a line of grunts
there on another children's crusade
and collapses at their boots, staring
up into the eyes of a soldier
who holds him whispering, *Jesus!*

Grunt

I'm a grunt on the front
on that line in the sand
in the war of the man
with the oil on his hands.
I'm a grunt, I'm a grunt!

I'm the first that they call
and the last that will fall
Can you see my history
in this land of the free?

Cutting costs, my company
sent my job overseas
so I'm stuck out of luck—
got no work, got no bucks,

I'm nobody's fool,
but I can't go to school.
See the rich set the rules
and use me like a tool.

From the hood, from the hills
train us all how to kill;
teach us hate like it's fate
takin' shit for the state.

What's their aim, it's insane,
I'm a number in their game.
Back home it stays the same,
I'm a grunt without a name.

Read the signs of the Times,
saying lies are not crimes,
and we're still cannon fodder
for the rich man's war.

But they can't keep us down,
cause the word gets around
the tail is wagging the dog
through another war's fog.

On the screen it looks fun,
in the sand they're real guns,
all those lives up in flames
with no glory with no fame.

Lay that pipe right from jump
so the man saves a buck
when he pays at the pump—
fill her up, caddy truck,
fill her up, caddy truck.

We built some stuff today,
we blew some stuff away.
We handed out some candy,
they blew up our humvees.

Torn apart by a frag,
I'm the body in the bag.
I'm the baby in the crib
blown to bits by a bomb.

And the sand drinks the oil
and the sand is never full
and the sand drinks the blood
and the sand is never full.

But they can't keep us down,
cause the word gets around
the tail is wagging the dog
through another war's fog.

I'm a grunt at that front
on that line in the sand
in the war of the man
with the oil on his hands.
I'm a grunt, I'm a grunt!

Testify

When I am called
by the authorities
to testify, will I
be able to look
the other witnesses
dead in their eyes?
Or will I look down,
jingling the coins
in my pocket?

Will I swear
an oath of apathy,
wanting only to be
left alone, to curl up
inside what I own,
where I can look
through the window
of my television.

When I am called
to testify, will I
shut up about the mouths
frozen open that tell
the story of some
poor slob who's getting
the crap beat out of him
even as I speak—
that's what he gets
for shooting off his mouth.

Will I meet my life
the moment it rises
outraged and stand
with it? Or will I
step aside and point

hissing, this is the one,
this is the one you want.
Well, will you?

From the Gulf War to the Gulf Coast and Back

That shadow on the wall in the photo from Iraq
is as much here as the wall and neither are
anymore but dust swirling along golden
flecks sticking to white winding cloth wrung
and hung to dry in the wind by red, raw hands
in Fallujah, where cups and shoes fill with sand
and scorpions guard their last drops of poison.

The wind rushing through the live oak ends—
there is no tree, only sodden debris from the flood
and the wind blows over where the 9th ward stood
whistling through the fence strung with beads,
through spokes of a bike riding half way into mud.
What folks are left no longer fish along the levee
for fear of eating fish that have eaten the dead.

In my hometown the stationary store on main street
has been turned into a recruiting office for kids
who have been left out of the *let the market decide*
who will get a new uniform and a used gun
and a bonus to fill up their gas tank with tears
to take one last road trip across the promised land—
from a rest stop they can see the bright lights
of the empire flickering like they will never end.

Silver Little Devil

I don't think
I'll get bumped off
on Good Friday.
Naw, not by that
15-year-old
baby-faced kid
on the subway
sitting with his bro
pitching lines up
the car to some babe.
He stretches to yawn
and thump—a thump
I've heard before,
his gun laying there
on the floor shining,
silver little devil.
He smiles, picks it
up and shoves it back
into his crotch and
goes back to flirting
while we turn back
to the screen of our
own newspapers.

The Real Survivors

Brain's been shrinking
since Neanderthals,
who buried their dead
cradled with flowers.

Some found with wounds
from Cro-Magnon flints,
progress thrown through time
as better spear-points.

Skulls of our own kind
from 300,000 years ago
have been discovered
with signs of scalping.

Then came civilization
and the first writings
hieroglyphs to tally
jars of oil and slaves.

Space became defined
as high rise and low rent,
down to storehouses
and separate races.

Figures one then zero
added up to empires,
spreading to the edges
of the last wild place.

A few real survivors
peer from the last green
wall of leaves, listening
as the chainsaws begin.

Service Berry

They used to call that
service berry, its bloom
a sign the ground
had thawed enough
for the settlers to bury
their winter dead,
he says as he casts
into the swollen river.

Also called shad-blow.
It flowers around
the time shad spawn.
Used to be so thick
they'd make a shoal
and you could see white
bass chasing them, striped
sides flashing in clear shallows.

There ain't crap here now
but crap. River runs too green
for its own good, the lawns
of the condos upriver
leaching off fertilizer.
We stare into the barrel
fire on a brisk Easter morning
after five days of gray drizzle
cleared to sun finally rising
over northeastern Ohio winter.

When I worked at Republic
I used to drive the molten
ingots through the flats—-
couldn't go no more
than 15 miles an hour
so they wouldn't slosh out.
It was 130 degrees in the cab

in the gut of summer but
it was better than the slag run,
snaking your truck down
that steep grade into the pits.
Lost 6 men in the 24 years
I put in my time over there.
Young guys mostly. No kids.
If your truck rolls down there
it'll combust in seconds. Poof.
Don't matter now anyway.
Work's gone. Pension's gone.
Insurance's gone. Beer's gone.

Swigging the dregs, he tosses the can
into the barrel fire, cracks the last
branch of a dead Christmas tree—
orange needles flaring and crackling.
One log thuds against another
in the dam's hydraulic, sucked
under and spit back up. *Yeah,*
the shad used to be so thick
through here this time of the year.
He casts and pulls bait through
empty river, *crap*. And casts again.

Rat's Teeth

Smug, bothered smile of the bank clerk
behind the bullet-proof glass, it's your fate
in her jeweled hands as you face the fact
of numbers which have deserted your account.
The two digits after your name have no line of fat
zeros after them to mark the round, empty hours
where you put your minimum wage with other
drones who have yet to figure out the game
or could not and gave up and became
the aluminum salvage entrepreneurs you pass
in the park with a nod as they collect empties
from businessmen on their lunch breaks.

But somebody broke blood all over the sidewalk
of the city today, and the crowd scurries around
for a look-see at what happens if one should fall
beneath the wheels that never stop turning.
He just jumped, someone said someone said
who worked in the cubicle right next to him,
and the contorted body in the suit and tie
and the broken pane up on the 14th floor
are what you're still seeing when the teller says,
I'm sorry but you'll have to see the manager.
yet another formality before being denied
a toe-hold in the economy. So you walk back out.

Main Street is one long, busy, four lane gullet.
And there's no throwing money down its throat
that will stop it from groaning *More, More, More.*
The insurance skyscraper's entrance swallows
shoppers and businessmen from the plaza.
Too many have too much to lose to stop
offering their inner life for another pay-check.
Sometimes it hurts like you're free, then you hear
that rat gnawing in the walls at night so it's teeth
won't incise through its skull, chewing wood, pipes
and wires that keep you connected to the white noise.

Heat-Wave Graveyard

Not knowing where I'll end up in this heat,
I detour the procession of necessary tasks
my fellow consumers endure to survive, like
the man hurrying towards the bank in a tight
suit, unbalanced checkbook in hand, checking
his watch, or the woman clicking from her beauty
salon weekly, careful of her coiffure in the swelter,
or the skate punk slacking on the shaded curb
of the convenience store, caging a pack of smokes.

When in doubt, I go straight to the graveyard
to sit a spell, reading stories the stones tell
as 99 cent vet flags flap on a weak breeze
over the small markers their country gave them
dwarfed by obelisks of the town's old money.
Swaths of un-mown clover blossoms nod a ripple
like delicate skulls, and the flashing undersides
of leaves nudge under the shadow of each other
like a flock of green wrens, a lulling hush
into which I whisper these worn down names.

Red mites scurry over the disintegrating white
marble of Nellie Sharp's urn, her beauty interned
underneath back in 1846. And I can't make out
the flagstone poem by old man McCann, lichened
over and stained by catkin fallings—something
that rhymes with *fate*. Maybe *mate?* or *late?*
She lays always beside him now these years later.
For all our hurry, our days will equal their stay.
But I feel safer hereabouts as everybody rests
in peace under one green lawn of contemplation.

I use a stone pillow for my sun-baked brain
and echo some of their names aloud again,
conjuring them to this balmy communion.

A poet's job is to converse with the dead,
and to translate the calligraphy of rain streaks
ruining down the faces of angels hovering
overhead, as well as the ragged starling's cackle,
and the bot-fly's lazy inevitable drone that peels
the seam of wavering afternoon open in its wake
as I walk, half-naked, talking to the markers as I go,
back to the daydreams that make up my home-town.

Blue Sky Beyond

The Blue Lake

One mushroom bloomed,
boomed in the middle
of the last century.
Then another and
another, shockwaves
rippling out to this day,
the fallout making
everybody expendable.

On the way out west
I stopped in Las Vegas
where billionaire Hughes,
tissue wrapped phone
in one hand, pointing
three inch nails out
the penthouse window
towards the testing site,
once ordered the president
to stop exploding A-bombs.

Mick, Ulster brother in arms,
on the lam from the Troubles,
told of Chloride, Arizona,
a dusty ghost-town run by
a skeleton crew of elders
along a main street that leads
to abandoned copper mines,
to a serpent mural painted
by a hippie across slag heap
tailings as a healing talisman.

Returning to the only store/
bar/restaurant in town
I notice a poem in the middle
of the menu—did someone

from here write this poem?
Well, Mister, the barkeep says,
peering over a cold mug,
there's two groups of poets
in this town. They meet here
every week on separate nights.

But you'll want to talk to Neil.
He's up scribbling most nights.
He's at Choir practice now.
A handful of elders inside are
a few steps away from the choir
eternal, wheezing out hymns
as he fiddles. I pegged him
by his Harley jacked draped
over the pew, thick glasses
and shock of grey pompadour.
Upon my entry the preacher
finishes rehearsal and launches
into a fire and brimstone tirade
about the depravity of Vegas
seeping into this god fearing town.

I sidled up to the fiddler.
You the poet? From the side
of his beak, *Yep, we'll*
talk about it after church.
He gave me a lift on his Harley
back to his miner's shack.
I'm not really much of a poet.
I'm a numbers guy, a math whiz,
but I wrote a poem on the bomb.
I started it right after the test,
sitting up on Mesa Alamogordo
watching that blue lake glow,
reflected in the overcast sky.
See, the heat melted the sand

into glass alive with isotopes.
What a close call it really was!
We were taking bets in the lab
behind Oppenheimer's back
on a possible chain reaction
sparking global combustion.
Meanwhile, Oppie stayed inside
his room translating the Gita
to relax, specifically Kali Yuga,
the last breath of the cosmos.

I played my bit part in the project.
Finished High School at 11,
entered MIT when I was 14—
of course standards were different.
Higher. Joined the team in '42.
The war gave us all work.

Been trying to write it out
ever since the generals dropped it.
Sitting up there, back against rock,
watching the blue glow of the lake.
Like I said I'm not much of poet.
Maybe you can help me with this.
I don't know how I escaped cancer
all these years, why I was spared?
The rest of the team is long dead.
First came the flash, then the light,
then the shockwave, then the black—
I didn't see my life flash before me,
just looked down through my goggles
at the veins and bones of my hands
then up at the stars, that light
14 billion years arriving right here.

To hell with them all anyway!
I went to Canada after the blacklist.
There were nine others who refused

to do Teller's H-bomb dirty work—
He was obsessed about commies.
They called me un-American!
I grew up in Nebraska's cornfields.
They split up me and my wife.
The thanks I get for ending the war.

That night up on Mesa Alamogordo
I felt like this could be the last gasp
of the earth before light collapsed
back to darkness. I actually prayed.
Me, a mathematician, and from the tips
of my fingers I had this vision
rushing like flood in an arroyo,
of all that Hiroshima destruction.
They showed us pictures, dissolving.
When I opened my eyes again
the blue lake was still glowing there.

There are ghost towns all around
the site, they moved everyone out,
but some came back and chipped off
hunks of it for souvenirs, putting them
up on their mantel. One piece even
got as far as Jersey and ended up
as a coffee table before they found it.
From up there I could see the seeds
the big boys at the Pentagon would sow
downwind of the fallout zone.
How many horrible blossoms
will we reap when it's all done?
The genie is out of the bottle now.
I saw those footsteps of power
marching the wide world over
till numbers of dead became numbing.
And I had a hand in all of it.

There is no stopping the military
once they saw what they could do
with their new toys, wearing sunglasses
in the bunkers like it was a day
at the beach, a very short day,
opening the black book of apocalypse.
They were so proud of its might
they would march officers out there
into the middle of ground zero
to show the power of the atom,
"This would be how Moscow ends."
Of course after all the leukemia claims
from families of the servicemen
they stopped that dog and pony show
and bulldozed the blue lake,
dug a big hole at the epicenter
buried it and concreted it over
just like they did at Chernobyl
except with inferior materials.
Not that it could ever be contained—
Pandora's box flung open to heaven,
Kali's fiery cosmos devouring mouth—
pick your prophecy it's all the same.
History tells us how civilizations
last for maybe a thousand years,
nowadays what with technology,
maybe no more than a hundred,
and we're making radioactive waste
that won't break down for 50 thousand.

I met Einstein too, absent minded
brilliance, he thought that people
had a conscience. I'm no theorist.
I deal in cold, hard numbers.
He sent Roosevelt a letter
describing how close the Nazis were
to making their own device.
Turns out they didn't have a clue

about fusion, but did have rockets
and once we beat them so did we.
After our device was deployed,
politicians promised the benefits
of atomic power in one hand while
hiding missiles behind their backs.

Sometimes I look at that blossom
frozen on the wall over there.
In those days Oppie called it
Kali's skirt. I guess it was that.
Ashes, ashes we all fall down.
When I refused to work for Teller
he got mad as hell, called me Red.
He wasn't even born here.
My resume was radioactive.
When it finally cooled off,
I came back down to Chloride,
ghost town for Christ's sake—
the shape of things to come.
I figure we have 50 years.
I go up to that hippie serpent
when the hummingbirds return.
Am I damned for what I did?
I can't see to write anymore,
but I can still see that blue lake.

I look into his blue eyes
blinking behind his bifocals
and see that blue lake wavering.
I leave him standing in the road,
drift of grey hair blowing
between dusk and darkness.

Atomic Milk

Out west, in the science-fiction
turned fact, late nineteen-fifties,
outside Las Vegas, city of neon
money dreams and T&A diversions,
in the salt flats of an ancient ocean,
mushrooms bloomed and boomed.

Downwind across the Midwest's
dairy pastures, cows munched
the green, green grass of home,
glowing through stomachs to udders,
and mothers drank extra milk
what with babies on the way.

Experts admitted it was better
after-all to breast feed than use
the formula my sisters drank.
So I sucked milk mixed with
strontium 90 and cesium 133
soaking into bones and skull.

In my cold war cradle I cried
for more, along with all
the other baby boomers
sucking what will live on
half-lives longer than life,
stronger stuff than even death,
our caskets time capsules future
generations will fear to open.

Tick

It's hard to resist a clock
hungry over your head tick,
tick, tick like that, it eats
away your hours as you sit
in the room and the room
does not shrink nor split
open, that's the worst of it,
tick, you think, you might
not eat again, food becomes
a way out you start to chew
your jaw clicks a metronome.
When you finally get home
and lay down it's no better,
tick, down to the stomach,
tiny gears tightening guts,
but don't worry now, work
works a hole in your head
that fills with ticks, digital
display helps no little bit,
the ghost of the tick is back
like the croc that swallowed
the clock—if only you could
think good thoughts and fly
away like Peter Pan, not want
and want like Captain Hook.

The Scream Flower

The functional sanity of this city
closes in on me tonight.
I just want to scream and have it echo.

But I don't. I stay shut up
in the stale rooms of my lungs
and look out at the towering lights.

Tomorrow, as usual, I will put on
my face like your face, and go out
and put in my hours without a stir.

But tonight all I can do is sit
in the dark and listen to the hiss
of the stars eating themselves alive.

Across the sickly river
at the institute of technology,
boys tinker with star wars.

Conclude we are insane—
hairless, fearful aberrations—
and we are no less awesome.

Because here we go again,
whistling while completing
equations of mass destruction.

Step outside the master plan,
stop, and the question remains,
how long can the mental sustain?

The brain itself is a flower,
a bloody thing stifled,
sputtering electricities of anger,

a blossom that lifts a scream
as silent as the tufts on a skull
wafting on a glowing wind that dies.

Attack of the Giant Cockroaches

Bruce the Nam vet says, popping open another beer,
turning his thousand mile stare across the high desert
just outside Los Alamos on our drive across America,

The world will come down to two, giant cockroaches
Godzillaed by radiation, stumbling towards each other
like men in rubber bug suits through burnt out city walls.
People will be long gone, screams fixed on the sidewalks
in some Pompeii like flash, or decimated by some plague
let loose by an enemy of the government who bought
the recipe for apocalypse from a greedy guy in a lab coat.

That's the way we're going. But the cockroaches will outlast
even rats and pigeons and fleas. They've been here since
before the dinosaurs—the dinosaurs took a dump on them
and they made a house out of it. Forget about pesticides.
They eat bug poison for breakfast. It makes them stronger.
The only thing that will stop them, they'll eventually run out
of our garbage till there are only two left—two really big ones.

Bruce smelled many napalm mornings, saw more than his share
of gore before they sent him back home to watch the running
tally on the TV, numbers numbing the public into a game
of acceptable losses to determine who will win in the end.
It became necessary to destroy the village in order to save it.

He goes on, *There's still a grunt way out there in a bunker*
with his finger hovering over a button, white noise blistering
his hearing, his eyes frozen open by G.I. amphetamines,
and the screen he's watching that he can never turn off
keeps rerunning the same cheap science-fiction movie:
Attack of the Giant Cockroaches, which always ends
the same way; the biggest one devours the other and
with nothing left to eat, starts to chew off its own limbs.

The End of *The Day the Earth Stood Still*

Open on a flying saucer on the lawn of the White House,
pan to Gort the robot standing shining potential as a missile,
cut to a clock, the hour Klaatu warned, stopped.
Cut to various citizens in suits and hats checking their watches,
holding them up to their ears.
Montage American laundry women taking clothes from machines,
checking inside, exasperated;
teeny boppers in the malt shop beating a dead juke box;
men standing next to big finned cars stalled at an intersection,
        arguing;
a row of dynamos still, crew cut managers scratching their heads;
a high heeled housewife trying to switch on the vacuum, the dish-
        tank,
and the cocktail blender all to no avail.
Montage the Arc de Triumph, traffic jammed, extras in berets
        shrugging;
London's Big Ben stopped; A cardboard façade of the Kremlin,
        dour soldiers
fending off dumpy woman at a bread line.
But no picture of Berlin's wall or Hiroshima's scarred skin.

Fade back to Gort standing still, and Michael Remy,
as Alien humanoid Klaatu, slicked back hair, chest out,
who has stopped the world in mid gear better than Ezekiel,
cut to Ronald Reagun watching at the end of his mind,
waiting for Death Valley Days to come on,
or the movie of him liberating the death camps,
or the commercial of him selling soap.
It's just a movie, Nancy tells him.
But he stands anyway and mouths the lines,
He has been sent by the League of Outer Space Nations
to bring peace on earth—by force if necessary.
Gort of the laser eyes stands behind him
and will reduce the world to a cinder.
The President agrees, decides for the rest of the world,
Ronnie mouths, Klaatu barada nikto!

and the populace rejoices.

Cut to Ronnie nodding, smiling, bobbling his head.
Cut to the redwoods—if you've seen one redwood you've seen
'em all.
Cut to a microphone, his voice laughing, *the bombing begins in five minutes*,
Cut to Bonzo, subpoenaed from Hollywood
after the Sputnik monkey's success,
a supposed Red and definitely an evolutionist,
cut to the preacher at the Raygun ranch, prophesizing
Armageddon,
fade up to Ron, putting on a ten gallon hat, standing tall,
taller than Michael Remy, taller than Klatu, taller even than Gort,
reach for the sky, Pardner.

Peace Comes Down

Peace comes down
to the human face
of the person sitting
next to you; you
turn and see her,
the Nagasaki girl
caught in that flash
snapshot of destruction,
face fused to throat,
who lived through black
rain, through shadows
of friends cast on walls,
to be with us tonight.
But she never grew
after that blossom fell,
it would have torn
the scar tissue—still
she smiles a little,
as we look at the flowers
of her dress, her eyes.
We carry her with us
as we leave and see
her sorrow in the face
of all the others
by candle light, the little
paper boats we launch
flickering into dark
onto the river of night.

Stars

Stars flicker as wild
eyes staring from forest edge,
as campfires of migrations
from original bonfire,
as jeweled necklaces
pyramid priests aspire to wear,
as lamps of shanties
skirting burnt out empires.

Called controlled explosions
by scientific thought, fusions
already dead by the time
naked eyes envision them—
the sky is actually falling
in a trillion to the tenth
power or so theory
postulates apocalyptic lengths.

Put two dozen monkeys in a room,
or actors in primate suits
on a movie set, let them
finger calculators for
Millennium until, *Eureka!*
The nut of fire
from the tree of night is cracked
open, and survivors
warm hands over nuclear ashes
wondering how bits
of thought became such
horrible mushrooms.

Tonight the stars are not spears-tips

pointing downwards, hanging
overhead, auguring fears.

They glister more than
diamond points of dice
rolled across black velvet
figuring random chances.
Tonight they swirl what
they stirred from the start,
those fiery exclamations
uttered from the heart's dark.

Blue Sky Beyond

Will we ever look skyward the same way again?
Now the New York skyline wears the scars
of the towers once there, and forever.
Witnesses said, *It was just like a movie*,
terror etched over and over across the blue fall sky,
across the TV screen of the mind's eye.
Will we finally be cured of our collective addiction
to slow motion, high-body count entertainment?
Or can we at least run the names of the secretaries,
janitors, executives, firefighters and police who died
as credits down the smoky screen at the end?

All week I've sung *O Beautiful for spacious skies...*,
wishing them and their families rest in that expansive peace,
beyond explosions, screams, sirens, howling crashes
and news updates, the space I sought while hiking
off the trail deeper in the woods to find
in the green and golden balm of sunset through the trees,
a place to pray, noticing in a shaft of sunlight
a delicate filament wafting up from a hemlock sapling,
and a long-legged spider tentative over brown needles,
a fragile passing confirming some permanence.

Then I notice someone else has been to this very spot
since the 9/11 wake-up call changed the world's spin.
This mourner has made a flag from twigs and bark,
with asters, the last flowers of summer, as stars;
and next to it, from the first red fallen leaves, a heart.
All week I've walked in the wake of the havoc
that hate and ignorance and greed can wreck,
trying to find answers under the rubble
but only coming up with a camp-made coffee-mug
found at ground zero inscribed, "World's Greatest Mom."

All week I've walked in shock, tearing at the sight
of the flag, remembering my father, Korean War vet,

and all of those who gave all for the rest of us.
But this is no flag-waving poem, not the red of anger
but the heart of compassion; not the white shroud
of dust on Wall Street, nor the white of fluttering
paper work, memos, pay invoices, and spreadsheets,
but the clouds and the blue sky beyond them
I see through a clearing of our native ground
as I breath and sing…*O beautiful for spacious skies…*

Whither Goest Thou, America

Toast to Mr. Rogers

What the flying hell!
I pull back the curtains
to the racket in the middle
of the night—a street
sweeper's rotating brushes
flinging the dead live
oak leaves over the lawn
of Kerouac's House, well,
the place he lived once
upon the time just when
he got famous and not
long after he took to drink
to deal with being proclaimed
the king of the beats and
all the scenesters and hangers-
on would harangue him
when he showed up sloshed—
like Buckley's snide sneer
on the firing line, Jack
unheeding his own advice
try never get drunk outside
yr own house. But he did,
stumbling the neighborhood,
singing crazy beat sutras
as he passed living rooms
enthralled by the blue eye
of cold war America.

The sweeper kicks the leaves
also over Mr. Rogers' lawn
who's been living here for
nearly fifty years now,
the mayor of the corner
of Shady Lane and Clausen
out there every day mowing,
edging, trimming and watching

as the fool world goes by.
They want to make that house
into some national landmark
cause he slept on the porch.
Hell, my dog sleeps on my porch!
He rarely talked to Jack but
still calls him *a drunk—and*
he was a queer drunk at that.
Him and his momma walked
all the way to St. Pete, he says
as he hands me oranges which
I squeeze into juice and mix
with vodka left in the freezer
as a house-warming gift. I lift
a glass for both from the porch
across from his tended demesne.
Here's to the American lawn.

Whither Goest Thou, America?

The Bodhisattva must first walk calmly through his danger, practicing charity and sympathy for the sake of all. He must retain his non-entity state and avoid fame...
if he retains fame, he will become valuable and no longer resemble the useless Tao tree no carpenter can covet. Being famous he will be hounded to his death; being a non-entity no one will want to use him.

- Jack Kerouac, *Some of the Dharma*

On the corner of Shady Lane and Clausen
stands the house where Kerouac was living
when on the On the Road was published
to widespread acclaim and overnight
he was proclaimed, King of the Beats,
a title he never wanted and came to regret.

I walk with the ghost of Jack Kerouac
through after-midnight streets of College Park.
America stays transfixed inside
where everyone can hide their suicides
in the blue flame of samsara
as Jack recites his beat sutra—
Whither goest thou, America
in thy shiny car in the night?
in your mad pursuit of happiness
did you lose true freedom's sight?

In the Nineteen-Fifties, mushroom clouds
bloomed in the cold war heart of the desert,
senators scratched out red list names
of everyone who did not think the same,
and the Russians launched Sputnik into space
as Jack walked towards inner peace—

He walks tonight past neatly fenced lawns,
past barking guard dogs forgiven.

He walks beyond any beatnik fame
refusing to play celebrity's game.
He walks past bigger and better cars
howling off to god knows where—
Whither goest thou, America,
in thy shiny car in the night?
In your mad pursuit of happiness,
did you lose true freedom's sight?

Who can know the world as it goes?
Who can hear the full moon's horn blow?
Who will heed the call and ride the rails
of boxcars echoing Orange Blossom trail?
O who will simply sit still and vision
this earth brimming with heaven?

I walk with the ghost of Jack Kerouac
through after-midnight streets of College Park
as America stays transfixed inside
where everyone can hide their suicides
in the blue flame of samsara
as Jack recites his beat sutra—
Whither goest thou, America,
in thy shiny car in the night?
In your mad pursuit of happiness
did you lose true freedom's sight?

Letter Left On the Kerouac House Porch

So as I sit still on the porch
in the faint breeze cooling
the outskirts of downtown
Orlando, gray moss swaying
from this 300 year old live oak
like American bhikku beards
that speak the long vowels
only stretched ears of Buddha
can hear, I ponder one word
to give at the end of this road.

One word as small as the seed
I once spit from this porch.
Smell those orange blossoms wafting
beneath the skyline of high-rise banks,
the tallest adorned with black horns
like Moloch, white church spires
below mirrored in its glass sides,
here on the whirl-pooling edge
of the Disney vortex — wheel
of samsara that spins all matter out.

I was broke when I came here
and never really made enough
dough for more than a good bender
though the estate sold the original
teletype manuscript of *On the Road*
to a football mogul for 2.6 million.
I never genuflected at the altar
of the almighty dollar when I prayed
down on my beat knees by the end.

But there is no end, only the golden
scripture unrolling and outlasting
the teletype, the live oak, and horned
cash cow. For what is the commerce

of eternity? Ask Walt Disney,
who plunked down his dream
of automated fun in the middle
of panther extincting swampland
that became an empire so rich
he could freeze-dry his remains
in a crypt under the magic kingdom.

What would Walt Whitman say,
who praises the live oak arms
upraised in steady ablutions,
as he hands out one carnation
with every Sunday newspaper
he's selling at the intersection
of Colonial and I-4 as America
rushes by towards Autogeddon?

The same meat wheel spun them
both to this sense realm.
The black and white cat sitting
on the car top lives also no less,
nor the chameleon scuttling over
dry leaves, stopping to tilt its head
and bat a translucent lidded eye
in a wink of awakening I saw
as the world refracted in a drop
of sweat dangling my eyebrow,
prism of light that flesh is heir to.

Open your eyes and close them—
there's being and nothingness
in a nutshell, but for that one drop
at heart, Avolokiteshvara's tear
that booze could not blot out.
That summer I would shower
six times a day, waiting for rain's
chant to cleanse the ignorant
steam of mind, listening for that

blatting of motion and stillness.

What good the teletype roll recording
the road traveled, or even this letter,
a goodbye as soon as a howdy do,
our comings and goings condensed
to a postcard of live oak and shack—
Wish you were here? Guess what,
dharma bum, you are! And the word
that bubbles up from the bottom
of spring-fed Lake Adair, this clear
breath bursting empty sounds…*still.*

Bull Lee's Advice

Things gonna change 'round here, my back
joints are creaking tapping out hits
of anesthetic sound on the fat cockroaches
that scurry through the guts
of this skeleton key machine.

You been watching them meat puppets
all night, humping lust hungry ghosts.
What you got, m'boy, is a little porn
hangover. Nothin' a pull
on your old bottle won't cure.

You're feedin' your chi into an orgy
of self-destruction. At least surf the net or
there's that new show, *Screw a Millionaire*—
the length some of these cravers will go
to gulp down a bucket of filthy lucre.

The news is always good for a laugh.
Networks put a serious smiley face
on the talking heads, dollar signs in their
eyes as baby eyes turn to double XXs
off camera, before the flies settle in.

You can watch the world get blown up.
Pretty soon you'll pay to pick
what cities you want blowed up!
What does the producer care.
He's poolside out in La-la land.

While out in the desert the white
lab coats are splitting DNA hairs,
and the big boys in their vultures watch
mass destruction behind every operative
they pay rolled and now have to take out.

But you, m' boy, got that cycle
accelerating from your balls to your brain,
bypassing the dusty heartbreak hotel
of your ticker where Kali the destroyer
reaches out her arms to you.

You wanna be grounded in her,
sink your tap root through death's door
deep into some fleshy dream,
so when spring comes
there'll be babies in the cabbage patch—

like your niece, spawned from
agent orange, who gets a new doll
every Christmas that falls down
and seizures. How's that for a slice
of hell you can wrap your mind around?

You know, Mac, most think
I'm nothing but a cranky old fart,
but I knew a little compassion
back in my day in spite of the regular
horrors that come with this model—

like knowing how to kill a man
with a simple #2 pencil
sharpened and pushed right through
the eye socket. That's a terrible
skill to have to live with.

But this monkey can pick bugs
from its neighbors back
as easy as puttin' club to the head.
Of course they crunch the bugs
like I'm crunching these words.

But the bugs give them worms,
and worms, I suppose, got their own

karma to work out through
the bowels, but then again I might
just be talking out my ass.

M'boy you wanna find your way
out of this mess of desiring,
sorrowful bones, you gotta get
inoculated with language
as a virus from outer space,
just keep talkin' yr way to silence.

Portrait of Ferlinghetti

His arched eyebrows seagull wings
hovering over a memory,
Ferlinghetti's eyes
glint aquamarine, Mediterranean waver
in the afternoon sun that streams
through City Lights Poetry Room window.

Whimsy ripples his salty beard
as he recalls, from the side of his mouth,
Corso's stunts—a Yonkers' guy
conjuring that Brooklynese Casanova's
staged heckling of *Howl.*
Now that was performance poetry!

The sun swells, a golden Napa grape,
glowing over the furrows and valleys
of his face as he gazes across
the glittering waves of years,
washing up here on North Beach.

The fire escape just outside the window
clambers down, the spitting image
of turn of the century
New York tenements
(rickety shadow continuity).
We had to buy the dump
to save it from the yuppies, he says,
lingo tolling the death of the city,
and small circles of poetry.
We'll all be ghost writers soon.

Like a smart-alecky gull
squawking over the prow
of Columbus' ships, *Turn back!*
Take apart the gold-plated engine
of the church. Let Christ come down,

he circles and settles
near the fire escape
with his sad laughter
and aquamarine eyes glinting.

Mike Salinger Explodes Time

Mikey's internal soundtrack makes
a staccato per cussing like the last
manual typewriter factory where
proverbial monkeys hammer out
linguistic equivalents of Einstein's
relativity into sub-atomic jazz riffs
he be-bop tip taps on his keyboard
reeling up strings of Gilliganed verbal
contraptions like his B Movie slimy
hagfish intelligence enhancement system
guaranteed to make you want to quit
your day job in cubicle hell, steal
a '55 noired up Packard and drive out
to Podunk town where you can still find
an all-night diner that serves coffee
so black and deep you can't help
but fall into the caffeine induced
synapse ricochet connect the dots
to trace into being on that far stool
his anti-disney hologram of a hepcat
in crew-cut and horn rims smoking
filter less cigs, sitting like the very theorem
for cynical reality until his dada eyes
spark with a prank and you look up
at the arms of the clock pin wheeling
little light galaxies in the well of night
when you look back he's gone so you
go outside and all that's left is a plume
of smoke and the night is a cup of coffee,
the stars dissolving swirl of sugar.

The Ego Show

The upshot of ego's ad
is how to finagle the angle
for the most face time,
since fifteen minutes of fame
has been cut down to
a three second sound-byte
pitch to cash in on the trend
and ride it to the peak
of what's hip and pop
for the most cha-ching,
to rack up the bling-bling
to hang on your bones.

See, you must play the game
to be beamed through screens
in every single mcmansion,
tract house, trailer or shack
across the wide world,
the world revolving around
the hungry eye, everybody
wants what they see on TV
and to be seen in a scene
to prove that they are real
even if only for a second,
one phosphorescent dot
burning, fading in the dark.

But there is still one tribe
out in the desert or deep
in the jungle who will not
let their pictures be taken,
their souls sucked out and
made into entertainment.
They'll refuse to sell out
at least not until the water
runs out, then we'll watch

on our flat screen mirrors
their little dots dissolve
faster than glowing plankton
drowned under an oil spill.

The weatherman reassures
that this heat-wave will end,
so we click away the remote
destroying another second
of existence, trying to find
a wildlife show somewhere,
cheetahs running freely across
grasslands chasing gazelles
while out in the parking lot
of the Cineplex where once
there were wetlands, ducks
on their way south, waddle.

So you never got to the top
and sit now in your cubicle
at work staring at dreams
down-loaded. One day soon
you will be given the choice
to take the implant and live
forever inside cyberspace
or die and stink like an animal.
It is going to pinch a little
and then the burning until
you're connected to the big
picture and you will no longer
have to live, but simply watch
your life looped in reruns.

Hummingbird

The saddest little bit
of the world
I've ever seen was
that cigarette butt
on the bottom
of Angie's platform
boot as she sprawled
on the stage floor,
her lipstick kiss
still smeared around
the white filter
the same color
over her crooked teeth.

But what she does
to get by is
nobody's business
but her own—
clunk, clunk!
she stomps up,
jiggling, "Nice
peacock," I point
to her tattoo blurring
into cellulite thigh.
It's a hummingbird,
she slurs a tease
into my ear
for the dollar,
green nest feather
folded long-wise,
slid into her garter.
She quick counts,
12 bucks and only
15 more minutes
before last dance.

I picture her kids,
sugar cereal mornings,
sent on their way,
then back to sleep.
At least they're not
running the streets.
They won't end up
out on the airport
highway like Destiny's
daughter. She used to
dance here too. If she
don't have AIDS
no one can get it.

I've seen shit
I can never forget.
What you want
to remember you can't
when I go, bro.
I'm coming back
as a hummingbird,
sucking nectar
from paradise
flowers all day.
They have no
natural predators,
their hearts beat
1,000 times a minute
like it's not beating
at all, like it's still
in mid-air, full
of sweetness, no one
can touch her,
the world unfolding
all around her.

Dancing with the Dragon

for Pat

Just under the surface
of waking, wavering
up between dream and
darkness, my sister's face,
vodka pale, floats under
a sheet of ice I break—
a blossom sinking,
drowning drink by drink
somewhere in Tampa Bay.
She's been bleeding for a year,
female problems, Ma says.
But the local sharks are too
drunk to tear her apart.
She lets them pull dully
on her limbs, leaving only
bruises she feels as she rolls
over in the litter box to the tune
of empty beer can clatter.

Who will give a kiss,
of forgiveness to melt
this cold world's dawn?
The boy who loved you,
hanging in the garage
with a bouquet of blue
flowers on his lips?
The father you fought
till he was laid to rest
with a whiskey kiss returned?
The fathers of your children,
dead drunk, dead, drugged out,
lobotomized, or unemployed?
The six children abandoned,

waiting for you to come home?

Once when you were sixteen,
I watched as you painted
a fluorescent green dragon
dancing with a maiden in purple
flowing peasant dress,
no knight in shining armor
anywhere in sight.
All the while you sang
sweet, clear, pure notes
Go ask Alice,
I think she will know...
notes I still try to reach
with my own songs.
When did you give up
trying to break through
the morning mirror's lying,
washed-out bitch made up
over sunken cheeks? You fall
through every excuse
to the bottom's bitter ends,
stomach acid eating your smile.

But your dragon charged
as that SUV when you
staggered out of the bar,
knocking you forty feet
out of your sandals
and into the charity ward
where they kicked you out
after three days, a pin holding
your femur together.
Charlie bought you a folding
lawn chair for a walker.
You smiled at that gift.
That same smile the maiden wore
as she danced with the dragon,

the same one you flash
to the bar ogres before
sipping vodka through ice
in the rock's glass, a last
kiss that melts water free.

A Cold Day in Hell

The vet leaning in line
alongside the shelter
holds his distended liver
through three coats,
knit hat pulled down
almost over blue eyes,
face frozen red and says
they said it would be
a cold day in hell
when I gave up the bottle.
I just saw Phil's friend,
I forget the guys' name,
he's that Indian though,
and he was curled up
around his jug and
I woulda killed him
for it, but he was dead—
blood freezes before
alcohol, but I guess
he didn't have enough
cuz there was one swig
left and I held it up
to the street light,
firewater, the Indians
called it when we first
traded it to 'em for furs,
but it didn't save him
and it sure as hell
was not gonna save me.
You gotta let me in,
it's a cold day in hell,
finally, man, it really is.

The Bard of Cleveland

for Daniel Thompson

What does a bard
give but his feet
of metered words
out on the streets
of cold Cleveland
moving heart to beat,
bringing daily bread
to people he meets.

A poet dies, you said,
every two years here,
but you're not dead.
I saw your ghost today
doddering down Euclid,
wearing a sky blue beret,
laying hands of words
on our wounded city.

You were no Saint,
but sang their praises.
You're just a poet,
voice for the voiceless,
working the homefront,
a hand to the homeless
in the parade of suits
who shun their faces.

Wont to crack wise,
your lines open doors,
your beard whispers peace,
you never asked for more.

The whimsy in yr eyes
belied yr simple power
that words can surprise
and poem become prayer.

The Strong Men Keep Coming

for Danny Solis

The bloodied Mex-American middleweight
staggering on the big stage in Las Vegas
who I watch on the bar's big screen
on Cinco de Mayo has just had his gloves raised,
he kisses both of them, signs the cross,
gives it all to God and smiles, the cuts
above, below, his eyes also smile and sting
with the good salt of a hard job well done.

And I slam down another shot of tequila
in honor of poet brother battler Danny Solis
who I went toe to toe with in the Boston Slam
for 8 rounds all even until I lost on points.
It takes a big man to cry and a bigger man
to laugh at that man as we laughed it all off,
like we laughed off the fierce tears of loss
you cried after your woman kicked your ass.

Laughed off also the tears of crazy Pat Storm
who called me sobbing a week before he died
on the mean streets to apologize for punching me
during that alley fight when you saved my ass.
We tell those tales trading shots of Irish whiskey
under your poster of Ali knocking out Liston,
putting a punctuation mark on the black motto
I am a man—and will not fight the yellow man.

I recall all those tough, poor immigrant Micks,
Dagos, Bros and Spics who fought their way
to the American dream of success only to stand
ready, waiting for the next man to enter the ring.
How we all took turns taking and giving our lumps,
punch by punch, until the world's big roundhouse

knock out laid us low—only get up again,
wiping blood, sweat and tears from our eyes.

Tonight I raise my glass also to Daniel Donnelly,
bare knuckle brawler who went 11 hard rounds
with the English Champ Cooper, no holds barred,
who took on beating on the Oul' Sod but finally
landed a right that shattered skillful Cooper's jaw.
Forgotten hero, he died broke and drunk in the gutter.
A doctor lopped off his right arm and mummied it red.
It was paraded around New York last St. Paddy's Day.

Ah, Danny, you know the strong men keep coming.
So here we stand after all these rounds of years.
Chicks dig scars, you told me, and if so I'm a champ,
up to my usual shenanigans, bobbing and weaving,
scraping together my night's earnings for a beer,
spitting out poems—it's not the paper their printed on,
not our voices, not even the proud bones of our skulls
that will last, but that we stood shoulder to shoulder,
that we fought the good fight to the very end.

And the Jazz Plays On

And The Jazz Plays On

Do you know what it means
To miss New Orleans?

The Mississippi deep keeps
that bass line thrumming,
that channel-cat tail swish, flood-log thump strumming,
the Big Muddy Mother of us all
carrying down in her strong brown arms
Ohio River valley hillbilly ballads
from West-By-God thru the Kantuck,
echoing 'round hollow, charcoaled bourbon barrels;
carrying down from Minnesota's, thousand blue-eyed lakes
clearly yodeled fiddle tunes,
carrying down from Missouri's Great Plains Basin
buffalo drum shaman chants,
merging them together with pedal-steel Tennessee twangs
across Gospel golden shores,
and Memphis empty whiskey bottleneck, silver fretted slides
that last swig washing down red
dust to dust sharecropper blues;
carrying down devil deals from Highway 61 crossroads,
Papa Legba in corn field shadows;
carrying down Delta juke joint, rusty fender cymbal crash,
cotton pickin' fingers scratchin' out boll weevil wobbles;
carrying down Arcadian accordion airs turned
up tempo Zydeco squeezebox
wheezing like a drunken gator,
and mosquito quick bon temps roulez reels
buzzing through Spanish Moss Cypress swamps—
Yes, the Mississippi deep carries all these American sounds
down home to New Orleans
where the beat began, listen:

You can hear it 'neath the shufflin' feet
on French Quarter's streets—
Yeah, I know where I got my shoes—

on the same swamp buckled bricks
where young Satchmo bottle cap tap, tip toe scraped out
his first tunes, no square foot level, giving a body that strut,
that hip pop roll just behind the beat,
that second line lag—
somewhere along the moon-walk levee
a trumpet plays as the last rays of sunset
hit this city below sea level
with one long, golden, high C note
opening evening's revelry
here in the Big Easy…

already on shady back streets
saxophones moan low, mood indigos
before Stagolee cuttin' contests
cut up into staccato laughters, *knocked-out loaded,*
and trombones intone
Come on over here Mama,
meet me with your black drawers on,
blown up by a tuba's fat, back beat blat
that punctuates 9th ward roots rap
echoing all the way uptown
where whiskey soaked poetry
riffs over Maple Leaf rags,
before wending back down to Congo—
Congo Square where the American Beat was born,
birthed by slaves every Sunday…

and that Jazz plays on,
the whole Crescent City buoyed up, swaying side to side
from the sheer weight and pull
of all those black, brown, high yella, and lily white asses
dancing together to Creole clarinets wailing,
boiling over like red beans,
to tambourines smacked on funky butts—
even demure parlor pianos have gone boogie-woogie bad,
cuz it's all loud and allowed, LOUD AND ALLOWED
here in New Orleans

and there's that clarion call, high C
arching over the whole wild ball again,
blowin' a cornucopia of meaty chops, squawks and growls

unto sweet melodies,
muffling down in layers, muffeletto style,
the low down on the down low,
Ponchatrain rain hushing over shotgun shacks
with tin roof vibrato, then huffling off
as sad, sexy viperish musings
of long gone Storyville, quadrilles trickling
jellyroll sweet, ebony and ivory kisses,
ceiling fan metronome saying,
this is where sultry became body,
on wrought iron balconies
where skin bathed under pouring milk moon,
cools by drowsy lingerie breeze,
as this city made of music whispers yes,
yes, wraiths walking xylophone bones
home to alabaster slabs,
and the Mississippi deep keeps
that bass line pulsing
through everybody's veins
as the Jazz plays on, one more tune
dawning in a soft, trumpet sunrise,
What a wonderful world, Oh yeah...

And the Jazz Plays On… Part 2

But that was before Katrina.
Now I gather these words and string them together
like muddy Mardi Gras beads
as faces of friends float by on the rising waters:
Lee, Burt, Kechaya, Jimmy Nolan, Andy, Dave Brinks
Felice, Renee, and Shawn D
all their whereabouts unknown after the flood,
after Hurricane W blew through as Round 2
from the Gulf War to the Gulf Coast
with its force 10 devastation of Bushit—
as Reverend Goat said,
New Orleans did not die of natural causes.
She was murdered by a perfect storm
of neglect, incompetence, and cynical national mentality
of everyman for himself
instead of we're all in this together,
neo-cons finally achieving American equality,
treating everyone the same way
they do black folks.

I turn on the TV and the reporter beams
his smile into the teeth of the storm,
making a name for himself.
Change the channel, the day after,
but the president is nowhere to be seen,
on vacation riding a mountain bike downhill
as the flood waters rise.
Change the channel, day three,
but the president is still out west
twanging out a redneck tune,
hiding Yale frat boy, blue-blood
under Stetson hat and Nascar jacket
while the flood waters rise.
Change the channel and finally on day five
the president flies overhead in Air Force One and says,
May God help them, since he sure as hell won't,

though his cohorts in cancer alley, petro-chemical plants
have helped themselves to thousands of acres
of storm-surge buffering wetlands
and gorged on tax subsidies while they gouge us at the pump;
and the vice-president has helped his former company
to cash flow diverted from rebuilding the levees
into blowing up Iraq,
Halliburton's coffers filling up
like sand in coffins, the same sand
that could have been used to bag the flood,
while the Feds blow another billion tax dollars
in the desert around Baghdad,
dropping smart bombs
with pinpoint accuracy on homes in Fallujah,
but unable to drop a bottle of water
into a child's hands in the 9th ward
or pull an old black woman off her roof for five days.

Change the channel and pundits ponder
why people didn't leave the city,
pundits who have new SUVs, homes on high ground
and high speed internet to warn them when shit is going down.
The same pundits who pick through debris,
and point clean white fingers at poor black folks.
Change the channel and news shows
white folks wading chest deep in the flood,
goods held high over head, and the caption reads,
Katrina survivors foraging for food.
Change the channel and news shows
black folks wading chest deep in the flood,
goods held high over head, and the caption reads,
Katrina refugees looting.
Change the channel and news shows
rescued dogs riding an air-conditioned bus to shelter;
Change the channel and news shows
children and elderly blacks packed
on the back of a rusty pick-up truck,
but does not show that truck turned away

by sheriffs at the Metarie city line,
as they wish they weren't in Dixie again,
and wonder how they became refugees in their own country.
Change the channel and the president's mommy says,
The refugees are better off here than they were before—
Let them eat Texas Toast.

Change the channel and the TV Talibangelical proclaims,
That Hurricane was the Hand of God!
Yes it was, but not to smite lesbians, leather bars and liberals,
but to tear away front page head lies
that all is well with the economy
and the war is almost over—
but you can't hide the weather
under a Bush anymore.
And the Talibangelical continues
his call for the End Times,
dollar signs in his eyes, for he has seen the profit
of scare-mongering, and verily his pockets have grown fat,
for he as poured fear into the ears of sheep
who bleat and repeat the hate they hear,
and he has blessed the missiles
that fall from heaven onto infidels,

while building himself an earthly mansion
of gated condos, and commanding the poor
to pull themselves up by their bootstraps
though they have no boots and stand
upon the rejected stones of the projects.
The meek, it is insured, will not inherit the earth
of this city, the have-nots huddle
in the shadow of the Superdome,
wondering what will become of their homes
while the have-mores plan casino deals,
as the dead grey arms of the live oak trees
bear witness to the Crescent City crucified.

But you cannot kill a necropolis,
New Orleans will rise again
from this solemn second line march
into the cemetery of the American dream deferred,
poor folks falling out in that awful heat along the way,
but cutting up on their way back home
through debris of shoes, rusty cars in trees
and past graffitied side of shattered shotgun shack:
I once met a gal named Katrina,
Never met a woman who was meaner,
She blew into town
Knocked all my shit down
Now I gotta deal with Fema.

Undefeated divas under fancy umbrellas
will lead the way, rolling their hips
the way the Mississippi does and always will,
confusing this premature death knell
because nobody down in New Orleans has ever been afraid to live
and so nobody down here is ever
going to be afraid to die,
as that jazz plays on—
listen, you can hear it, as flood waters recede,
the spirit of Satchmo, grabbing Gabriel's horn,
and wailing from the cradle of American civilization,
this call for a new heaven, and a new earth,
where the saints really do go marching in.

Key West Coastal Park Sculptures

I.

A man shape, torqued together
from wraps of steel, steel
forged by men sweating
in factory flats,
and cooled long ago, hangs
soaring spread-eagle free,
almost, of the chains
once used to lift
cracked engine blocks
from car wells
of rusting hulks

A man shape hammered
into coppery leaves
of acrobatic glee
by some artistic offspring of the mills
working here in the Keys,
far from ball bearing gray winters
and the fate of one of those lifers
grunting shifts, who barely made it
off the line in Gary, Detroit, Toledo,
Cleveland, or Youngstown,
and who would never dream
of pounding metal
in his free time
into any other shape
but anger.

The man shaped prison bar chest
unfurls in mid breath, in mid air,
as if the aluminum winged-heart
readies to scrape out
over palm-serrated sky—
bound only to be
corroded away by

salty spray
into flakes of sun.

II.

A marble bust of Mariah
her sea-foam braids
carved crystalline
into thick cascades,
woven together
as by lute-versed fingers
of some daughter
of Lesbos,
and pulled back
from her alabaster,
pink-veined face
that tilts ecstatically
still, eyes closed
to the sky's
azure mirror,
no body below,
simply the sea's
deep blue
orgasm.

III

I sit in the lone, tall shadow
of Mister Train Tracks
twisted up into a cocky strut.
Someone has given him
some poppies to hold
on his hip. Ah, Whitman,
lover of blossoms and steel,
this is how progress stands
in America,
proud in its junk,
given to sea-breeze grooving
over beveled bones.

Thank you, Mister Rust,
for blocking
the tropical burn
from my skin. The sun
haloes the welded loop
of your head like, ah,
what else, a sun flower.

IV

From a mound of fine ground white sand
stuck with hundreds of up-ended blue bottles
comes this message of emptiness, the wind
when you lean close, whistling sheer azure sky.

V

And the twin-headed
blue-gold wind vane
high on a 20 foot pole
turns and points from
where the breeze blows as
he prows towards there
just above ocean's horizon.
His yellow-gold twin head looks
back from whence they spun,
in the wind's wake, seeing
the world wide current togethered.
The span of their shadow
hovers over orange tufts
of beach grass like the wings
of one of those huge tern
from the Far Tortugas,
those prevailing wind gliders
that only land to mate.
So these partners turn
from their axis, wedding earth
and sky over sun-burnished sea
to the four winds – oh, how
I would spin when I was a boy

until I was dizzy as I am now.

VI

A sea-blue steel plate,
blowtorch cut outline of a woman
waves from the channel's
break-wall edge,
waves to biplanes' fly-by buzz,
to jet ski's macho ripples,
to sailboat's clinking tackle
and wine glasses toasting.
She waves hello and
goodbye to the noise,
of what passes over waves,
over our gentle graves,
bon voyage, she waves

She maketh me to lie down
on the narrow beach
beside this lapping, ready
to be bleached out
like an empty shell
and crushed underfoot
by others who come
and go from this shore…

And still she waves,
wishing well
to whoever, herself
neither coming nor going:
blending into sky
but for the orange flowers
that glint through the slits
of her cleavage.

VIII

Superimposed over a field of sun-brittle weeds
and the crumbling bricks and mortar

of Fort Taylor's walls,
a mesh wire ballet dancer leaps
into wind, racing against
gravity, and, at least for today,
suspended in the wild,
blue yonder's embrace.
This is how iron life
springs from the ground,
coils up and holds here
as the blood exhilarating
my body suddenly
standing reddens
and rusts
with each
breath

California Evening Waves

for Monica

The whole visit ends up
overlapping in yet another sunset
we just missed, traffic jammed
on the Marina del Rey causeway,
but see now as the lingering afterglow
of the sky's bright, blue orgasm,
A corona of last rays unfurling fuchsia
through the L.A. haze better than
any Hollywood ending.

A pelican flops below
the surface of the channel
where dusk and water merge,
as a scull scrapes homeward across the bay,
the captain barking strokes,
and a trawler plows past,
net rigging lit-up with strings of fiesta lights
as houses flicker on around the hillsides
like ancient campfires.

Last night our bodies formed a reef
dreams fanned from, long strands
tugging entwined in the dark
current of sleep after love,
the surf of breath hushing
over us, memorizing
our shapes to their depths.

Now on the other side
of the break wall's wash
of cold, cobalt swell,
the beach shivers
Pacific vastness

down to gentle laps
before the next wave
that started rolling
days ago, far out,
kisses the shore here
and here and here…

Venice Beach, Florida

I've escaped Cleveland's usual
winter from hell cold burn
to sit and stare at the blue sea,
not a glossy color postcard,
just what's left of one wave
cupped in a child's hands,
dripping from her fingers, wonder
enough for one day endless
as the old man shuffles by
in the surf on his last legs,
checking his watch and pulse
then turning back to scatter
a flock of gulls doing yoga,
white down breeze furrowed,
wave froth blowing back,
past the grey-haired couple
smiling dentures as waves chew
Venice Beach, nicknamed
God's waiting room by locals,
the average age here is 67,
he laughs, sifting through drift
for shark's teeth to send back
north to grandkids who hold them
up to grey February light,
imagining slow swimming death.
Today the sea looks like nothing
but exactly the expanse it is
The Mexican worker, legs dangling
from the wall, looks westward
across the Gulf towards home
and sighs into the waves' breath
that started rolling days ago and
exhales now on this shore we share,
no longer strangers by the sea.

Cleveland Sunset

One drop of Lake Erie
wave crash over broken
concrete break wall
flares up and fills
with spring sunset
anointing my forehead
so I no longer see
hazy downtown skyline
along the western horizon,
but gaze through ozone
back to the beginnings
when the forest city
was still mostly forest.

That one drop coheres
around a child's laughter
as she throws worn stones,
an outboard engine's whir
and a black lab's barking
as he snaps at dead carp,
stinky wave foam, goofy
stare happy that we are all
happy now on the shore
for our winter's over party
here in North Collinwood.

The grey cast iron lid
slid over us for months
has finally been lifted,
so the thawed land laughs
green maple leaves and smiles
daffodils and dogwoods.
My own first memory smiles
back at me now, my sister
swinging me at the end
of 148th street playground,

out over the face of the lake
into the blue sky and back
earthwards to the grass again.

Today the Lake's face ripples
and cross hatch shimmers
all the way to Canada as I
glance back at the dissolving
skyline, breathing in a tinge
of arctic ice shelf exhale
as it shears off from the circle.
Eastward the CEI smokestack
belches high sulfur coal through
long broken scrubbers, the same
plant blamed for the great blackout
along the East Coast in 03,
the sky overtaxed by the latest
clean air act smokescreen.
And somewhere a cow farts
out in Amish country and starts
a hurricane in the South Atlantic.

As a boy I could not swim
in Lake Erie now matter how
hot the summer sweltered
because of the mercury run off.
In those days we would joke
how you could use the perch
for thermometers—my hometown
became fodder for comedians
the "Mistake by the Lake,"
the Cuyahoga River Burning,
the burning hair of Mayor Perk,
the flats still burning three shifts
through the rusty, hazy dawn
of rush hour's heavy metal jam.

Now the Lake is everybody's
toilet bowl, e coli overflow
from the sewers of the suburbs,
dead zone in the middle
spreading closer to the shore,
but not yet – that one drop,
startles my third eye awake,
past d a levy's depressing
forehead bullet hole dead end
look at Cleveland's doldrums,
washes my vision 12,000 years
to mile thick glacial white wall
seen across the melting waters
by mound builders who nomaded
up from the Mississippi Valley
this far north through hardwoods
once so thick a squirrel could leap
from these shoreline treetops
all the way down to the Ohio river
without ever touching the ground.
A jet ski blares past and its wake
laps a too green bloom of moss.
I look back at the City and barely
make out the ghostly Terminal tower,
telling edifice of crumbling civic glory,
once the second tallest in the world,
finished just as the Depression sent
Cleveland into second city status.

Hoot, hillbilly brother, yodels down
The cliff on his lone day off
from the rust proofing shop,
scrubbing grease from engine guts,
from between his fingerprints
like his old man did in Ironton
and hands me a cold beer and asks
for a hand pushing slabs of old road

over the edge to save his house
from the soft, relentless wave's teeth.
Meanwhile two girls are building
what they're calling Fort Forever
from red bricks that once paved
the streets of the old neighborhood.

No, it's not the end of the world
but you can see it further inland,
past Bratenhal's boathouse condos,
in East Cleveland vacant tenements
and boarded up crack-houses.
At this point, Hoot posits, we are
only moving deck chairs around
on the Titanic. But that doesn't stop
the girls project. This could be,
she says holding up a brick
with a hole in it, a caveman's TV.
Put that one on top, she asks me.
So I do and she hands me another.
Then another. What else to do
but keep building this break wall
from the ruins of our broken city
as the waves keep rolling in
and the lake darkens with evening.

Cleveland Style

Dumpy squat my Slovenian side,
but nervy quick when they'd skip
that little hitch of 1 and 2 and 3 and
turn the Cleveland Style polka
across the shiny, slippery floor
of Rahar's Hall Saturday nights,
men dressed in their *Full Clevelands*,
pastel colored, wide lapelled leisure suits
with matching white patent leather
shoes and belts, flowered rayon shirts
open to show St. Christopher medals
given when they left the old country.

Fueled by Carling's Black Label beer
and Canada Club whiskey high balls
or sweet Ljubljana wine for the ladies,
they slapped their shoes across the floor
whistling and yodeling, blowing off steam
from shift after shift at the factories,
whirling through the "Beer Barrel Polka,"
"She's Too Fat," and "Just Because,"
my Grandma's favorite, her worn feet
stuffed in heels, varicose legs balancing
her body finally free of the drill press grind
in that 1 and 2 and 3 and swing.

But all the old Slovenians are dying out.
Last year at cousin Billy Zallar's funeral
on 185th street, where they ran their used car lot,
they played Frankie Yankovic and the Yanks,
the band he drummed for back when Polka
filled every living room from St.Vitus through Euclid
on Saturday nights and Sunday afternoons.
They buried him with his sticks in his hands.
And my mother, still dancing with her club,
The Forever Young Tappers, takes my hands

as we cross the parking lot after the wake
and leads me, one more time in that hop
and skip of the Cleveland Style polka.

Warren Rolling

Rolling down the road last Saturday Night
in my '79 Pontiac Grand Am,
got 400 horses, she's barely street legal,
gonna show those cruisers just who I am.

> *Goin' down I-90 doin' ninety,*
> *the cops they're on my tail,*
> *they threw down them jags*
> *to puncture my mags,*
> *sent me rollin' headlights over tail.*

Learned how to run them ridges down home
with a trunk full of ol' moonshine.
Richard Petty ain't got nothin' on me,
I'm just too fast to do any time.

Rollin' down that hillbilly highway south,
ain't seen them mountains in years.
I'm goin' so far back it'll take ten bucks
to send a postcard to me there.

This one's for my cousin Warren,
who knows how to make engines sing.
Hope he's rollin' through the hills of Ohio,
hope he don't blow no piston rings.

The first car sputtered
into their neck of the woods
back in 1896—word of it
had been spreading for weeks.
My kinfolk all came out
to the county fair grounds
in their Sunday finery
and filled up the stands
to watch that tin lizzy

spin round and round
the horse track whirling
up a cloud of red clay dust
that covered the ladies' hats
and the men's starched shirts
and Zelma's nine-year old wonder.
Fast forward 85 years later
as she sits at the window,
curtains billowing the breeze
of another car swishing past
on alternate route 550.
She scratches white pad
with pencil stub, adding
how many pass by an hour
on any given day, memorizing
the Old Testament between.
There are more and more
cars passing by every year.
Out back her great-grandson
Warren has got his head stuck
down in the engine well
of his 4 point 06, 8 banger
Chivlay Capris, polishing up
the chrome dubilator, tightening
down the 3 flanged javis
all afternoon all summer long.
On the Goody's Headache powder
demolition derby racing team,
he'll be bolting down the hood
and welding shut the doors
for Saturday night's main event
when that little valley becomes
a roaring heavy-metal hippodrome.
He'll climb through the window,
strap in and tear around the dirt
track in circles, going nowhere fast,
trying to hit and not be hit and be
the last car running before

he bursts into the grandstand wall
in a cloud of red-clay dust, smoke
and applause, wiggling free
from the debris and kicking
a flaming tire across the finish line,
a cigarette down to the last ash
dangling from his lower lip.

Yeah this one's for my cousin Warren
who knows how to make engine's sing
hope he's rollin' through the hills of Ohio
rollin' in his sweet baby's arms.

The Last Hillbilly

Alas a hillbilly, I once had a home
in the hills and the hollers where my ancestors roamed,
in the peaceful green valley where our bones we did lay,
but the steals of the bankers took that away.

We hailed from the highlands, the glens and the downs,
crossed the big pond to escape from the crown,
lived with the Shawnee and learned of their ways,
but the steals of the bankers took that away.

We hunted and fished and used all that we killed,
wove our own clothes and tilled our own fields.
We bartered with our brethren on festival days,
but the steals of the bankers took that away.

Along came the rails to carry off the coal,
to clear cut the forests to feed to the mills.
They took all the land we had nothing to say,
the steals of the bankers planned it that way.

We dug in the mines and coughed the black lung,
sweated in the mills till the long day was done.
To slave for our pay was the way we could stay,
the steals of the bankers kept it that way.

Just like the Shawnee we once had a home
in the hills and the hollers where my ancestors roamed.
But my friends and relations were gone yesterday,
the steals of the bankers took them away.

When I'm a skull and the Great Spirit calls
to the land of the blessed where the brave never fall,
to the peaceful green valley and the cool forest glade
where the steals of the bankers can never invade.

Grandma Corn's Crow Story

Crow caws crack like fall corn stalks
across misty, harvest furrowed field.
A murder perches on bare oak edge
ready to scavenge last kernels of sun
hardening in Grandma's gray body
laid down, whispering bleached leaves.

Crow caws crack like kindling burning
in Erie campfire along the Cuyahoga
where Grandma stirs a pot of mush
in the chill morning reminding children
how brother Crow, once white plumed,
tried to devour the kernel of the sun.

Flying higher and higher on a dare,
beak clapping, his feathers charcoaled
as he flopped back down to cool earth
where his burnt call still carves the air.
So go give him a taste of the pot lickings
after they cool off to balm this lesson.

Down Home

They called my Daddy Arkansas,
not cuz he was from down yonder
but on accounta his *Ahia* drawl
and Lil' Abner boots, work boots,
and rolled up carney jeans he wore
walking the halls of Collinwood High
with Dagos and Slovenians
at the bottom of the pecking order.
Mom's parents never forgave her,
at least you coulda married a Polack!

After he died the death of a salesman
broken-hearted, we found a tape of him
trying to flatten out his mountain twang.
Some boss told him nobody would ever
buy anything from a stupid hillbilly.
I can fake his hill-jack lilt pretty good,
spending summers with kin down home
not far from Ulster ancestors' bones
making up half the Graysville cemetery,
hill town not shaved off by Big Coal yet—

our home place unpinched by freeways
or stitched over with towering power lines.
Take I-77 to the 4 lane to the 2 lane
to where the pavement turns to gravel
to the wheel ruts to the foot path
to the deer run up to the log cabin
where spinster aunt Sade McNiece lived,
where ghostly fiddle tunes still curl
down hollers like *Beagle Chase the Squirrel*
and *Pollywolly* rolling high lonesome yodel.

The same tunes follow Appalachian spine
from Red Mountain in North Alabama
through Georgia, Tennessee, North Cakalaka,

West-By-God, Virginny, Western Maryland
Pennsylvania, New Yawk's Adirondacks
into Vermont's Green and continuing up
through Granite State's White mountains,
under the Atlantic, cresting in Ulster, dipping
into the Mull of Kintyre, and rising in Scotland,
tribes migrating that range for Ice Ages, singing,

or yelling blue naked streak downhill
raising hell on Romans, Danes, and Angles
before retreating into forests until
sacred groves were cut down, and we were
converted and cleared from the highlands
and stuck underground to dig in coal mines.
We were never purely Celtic but mixed
with African Picts, Vikings and Spanish sailors—
ghosts of Cherokee haunt our blood,
Shawnee we married pulse through our veins.

My Daddy's people learned the three Rs:
Reading, Writing and Route 77 North,
following the concrete river to factories
for jobs after the depression in war plants.
The joke goes, why are all the hillbillies
in heaven chained up? Because they try
to go back to the hills every weekend.
But now there is not much left here
in this rust bowl, but a dead mill
in the middle of Cleveland's Flats.

My Daddy never made it back down there.
He'd been everywhere, man, just like
the song his hero Johnny Cash sang,
from Korean War south seas Navy tour
to road trips across America selling
dental equipment with his Irish smile
and corny humor and a dream of building
his own house not far from that Cabin,

of walking those red dirt back roads,
and singing songs that recall his home,
down in Coolville on the banks of the Hocking.

Chagrin River Meditations

1.
Droughty Chagrin River
shows its spine,
ocher shards of shale baking
under blue flame
of summer sun kiln,
while the valley's broadleaved
poplar, sycamore, and cottonwood
ribcage exhales upward
from this thin, green pulse,
where I wade, following
the blue heron's
slow glide.

2.
Summer river smell
churned up by dam fall,
sides of carp roiling
like muddy suns.
Indian chewing gum
vines and new willows
on the bank remind
body to be lithe.
Heron flaps up and calls
off Chagrin shale cliffs
that hearken back
to the inland sea
of millenniums ago,
before traffic rushed
up above on River road.
Striders dart and skate
across the skin of the flow,
startling the surface awake.

3.
Learning to be as keen
and direct
as the Kingfisher
perched
on a branch
over log-jam beaver pool,
eyeing shadow
slivers flashing
before drop diving
straight in, under
and back up
as if it never left,
silver flashing
in its beak.

4.
The shiner shapes
to the channel currents,
the red-tail hawk gathers
Lake effect thermals
under its wings,
and my bones heal
together with this breath.

5.
Is it possible to go with the flow
and not be a dead fish,
to breaststroke against the current,
blood pumping through body,
climb the bank and shed thoughts
like old skin as a snake curls
this question across the river?

6.
Sitting on a boulder,
middle of the flow,
this is solid real,

these swirling waters
turn time's wheel
beyond what I feel.

When that glacier
sheered in half
late last summer
I breathed its exhale
across Lake Erie,
cold end of world.

I sit in my bones,
though mineral calls
to mineral stones,
web filament glints
on first spring breeze,
roar of river freed.

7.
Chagrin's green tongue unrolls
a fugue of tones, the rapids
flash lightly and churn over
glacial till boulders shoved
down from Canada eons ago,
ice age melting into history.

Cool undercurrents roil up
earth debris carried downstream
into thrum of deep sloughs
where carp dream ancient seas
congregating around gas beads
bubbling between shale fissures.

I rise pulsing from swimming,
the river's pulse streaming
down the curves of my body
and lay down straightened bones

to let the sun bake my body,
emptiness wind's breath echoes.

8.
I sit staring from a poplar log jam,
river of leaves hushing the valley's brim,
as a waft of cottonwood down
settles over the slow current
humming summertime, summertime

9.
Still still here
before I enter
within hearing
of freeway hurry.
There's somewhere
I have to be soon.
Still still here.
And when I'm there
I will stand as this.

10.
First dusk of fall.
My breath puffs
over silvery flow
of Chagrin, steelhead
riffling shallows upstream.
A V of geese honk down
skidding along a slough.
Quiet. No mosquitoes.
No sound but the freeway
as gray wings of Winter
unfold over sunset.

Chagrin Song

September Chagrin river swells
after last night's storm and already
yellow poplar leaves swirl
just under the cool, green current.

Rippling lightly up under
the basswood's fat leaves
the Autumn sun reflects
from boulder rapids.

The only other sound besides
the chirring of summer cicadas
high in the tall poplar trees
is the cast of a fisherman's plop.

A rock bass fingerling flashes
in the Chagrin's autumn pool,
its striped sides a good sign
through clean shallows.

From a poplar branch overhang
fifty feet above, a kingfisher plunges
under the green sheen of the sloughs
and pops back up silver flipping its beak.

In a boulder eddy, a coiled water snake
swallows a mad-tom catfish bigger
than its head down stretched gullet
both still breathing under autumn asters.

How to still the whirl
of the world still eludes me
but for this single leaf fall
widening outward everywhere.

Love Song For Cleveland

Rusty guitar strings picked by worn down, grimy ridged factory
fingers
greasy with city chicken twang out this tune,
like northbound train chugging up from Alabama red clay
sharecropper days
(and white sheet nights), picking up speed lickety-split,
then kicking into rockabilly freeway go, man, go
from them hills and hollers of West By God, rockin' up routes
77 and 71,
before crashing beat on North Collinwood, Lakeshore
Boulevard back porch,
my old man blowing summer harmonica breeze, spitting gritty
soot from the Flats
washed down with fruit jar shine and cold bottles of POC—
this love song for Cleveland could easily be the blues...

that same Labor Day off breeze carries accordion squeezes,
Slovenian beer-barrel polkas yodeled through Rahar's hall,
Campo basso lullabies cascading down Murray Hill,
Bohunk Old Brooklyn shadow of steel mill waltzes,
and forlorn, concertina airs recalling Achill Island,
the fugue of all those tunes spreading out this evening
and settling over carp-back burnished sunset across Lake Erie
from western Firelands eastwards to Appalachian foothills
from the Heights to the Flats and all those blues between—

the gloaming pierced by the eerie yowls of panthers
that once lurked through this Forest City
when it was still a forest, where wolf howls echoed the ridges
above elk-buffalo game trail that ran just the other side
of the East Shoreway's hurry and screeching coal train over
rusty tracks,
the same song lines the Erie tribe followed
to the Cuyahoga's swampy mouth,
can you hear their campfire hunting chants?
This love song for Cleveland could easily be those blues.

Can you hear Lorenzo Carter's Under the Hill Boys
swatting singsong malarial flies and wheedling brandy fueled
        fiddle tunes
that skirl into Navies' ditties as they dug the Erie Canal
at the foot of Superior Avenue, the tune merging
with shanty Irish rowdy dowdlings rowed back from Whiskey
        Island
to the Angle, sodden gut string reveries for the oul' sod?
This love song for Cleveland could easily be those blues—

blasted by 1955 Lake Boat freighter horn up Collision Bend way,
clearing the air above swinging, singing bridges into a swirl of
        seagulls
rising from from slag heaps, to reveal rusty red pellets glowing,
Cleveland's pot o' gold hidden under sulfurous clouds of
        Industrial Revolution—
at one point 15 tons of stuff per year was dropped here
on 9th Street docks where Gramps stevedored
fresh off the boat from Slovenia after the First World War,
unloading the Mesachbe range iron ore forged into steel,
steel that built this city, this country, hell, the whole world,
from safety pins to I-beams to the very hull of that freighter.

Listen to the din of Titan Mills whistling shifts,
silenced now, smelteries not even smoldering, rollers still,
dinosaur hulks groaning in the wind, collapsing
into piles of rust, or blow torch cut up and sold to China—
"Shanghai-ed!" curse the last union dock men
into their boilermakers, creased hard working, drinking faces
laughing off lacquered Tremont bar surface reflecting
bowling ball trophies golden
as the suns nobody sees for months on end.
Soon their blast furnace guffaws will also fall silent—
this love song for Cleveland could easily be those blues…

ghosting along empty Euclid Avenue Corridor,
past bustling post-war prosperity shoppers
through May Company, Halles and the Arcade,

before it picks up the squeal of St Paddy's day bagpipes on cold
March wind,
catches that hip-hop beat at the intersection of East 55th street
and raps it all the way to Severence Hall where violins
pull as sorrowful as Warsaw ghetto kaddish,
then wends it up Cedar Hill where a Polish Clarinetist from Parma
plays Duke Ellington's 'Single Petal from a Rose'
in an Irish Émigré Jazz club…

until it arpeggiates down Mayfield Road to Little Italy
where old paysans strum mandolins
as mournfully beautiful as the Virgin Mary
pinned with dollars parading the Feast of the Assumption,
before finally wafting out again from the shores of Euclid Beach
Park
where my parents first met and kissed,
dancing in the pavilion to big band swing,
I listen now as it rolls out across the lake as low grey clouds
roll in like a chorus of steel cellos droning
the hundred shades of gray that pall over Cleveland
so gray it's the blues—

Gray of winter's dead snow, sooty piles that line streets from
Kinsman to Ohio City,
gray of the aluminum shovel that sits by the front door year round,
bleached gray of beer can crushed during some hot night, late
inning Indians' loss
and tossed into unshorn hedges as bare gray as tree line on opening
day,
gray stink of shad kill along Edgewater Beach in Spring

gray of cinderblock coal bins along Train Street in Tremont,
gray of 55-gallon drum of rainwater on the back of a gun-metal
pickup
stuck with four flat elephant skin tires
beside a dull steel corrugated warehouse off concrete potholed
Waterloo Avenue,

gray of the Shoreway where the road melds with the sky and the
    Lake
so you can't tell what time of day it is,
if Picasso had a gray period Cleveland would be it,
gray faces of tract houses from Euclid to Garfield to Lakewood
glowing by dawn's first light, set and determined to meet
    another day,
gray of Harvey Pekar's hang dog face staring
into empty file cabinet at the VA before walking from dingy bus
through Cleveland Heights twilight,
gray of Daniel Thompson's Whitmanesque beard as he harangues
the specter of Rockefeller's empty tomb in Lakeview,

gray of the gray haired, mustached babushkas of Slavic Village,
gray of the frost on the lawns of Shaker Heights,
gray of Terminal Tower in the fog,
gray whirl of pigeons rising from Public Square blending with
    evening,
gray of summer thunderheads rolling in off the Lake
that give way to a perfect blue sky, high summer day in July,
come March and its long march of gray
you'll be on your knees begging for that blue sky day,

gray skyline in November that still calls me home
to hymn all these penumbras, that holy light
where dark of night meets gray of day,
gray of the last plume from the last stack of the last plant
still burning in the flats, the plume rising
like the ghosts of all those mill workers,
and though there is no sun that flame burns on
this love song for Cleveland
could easily be those blues.

About the Author

Ray McNiece is a true native of Cleveland, Ohio, with family roots in Appalachia and Slovenia. His great great grandfather was a member of the 64th Ohio Infantry Division who fought in the Civil War, and his father was a decorated Korean War Veteran. He has been active in progressive politics and the peace movement since his days at Ohio University.

He has authored two books of monologues based upon his solo theater pieces *Us? Talking Across America* and *Dis–Voices From a Shelter*. He is also the author of four books of poetry: *The Bone-Orchard Conga, The Road that Carried Me Here, Song that Fathoms Home*, and *Wet Sand Raven Tracks–New Haiku.* With the band Tongue-in-Groove he has created two poetry musicals–*Mouth Music* and *A Rust bowl Hootenanny*, and produced two CDs: *Mouth Music* and *The Road that Carried Me Here*. He collaborated with Shawn D. Jackson to stage the theatre work—*Homegirl Meets Whiteboy*. With Larry Smith he co-edited the international anthology of contemporary Buddhist poetry, *America Zen*.

Of his first solo theater work, *Dis*, *Edinburgh Scotsman* commented "McNiece's characters are acutely observed, the speech patterns and mannerisms perfectly caught." London's *Stage and Television Today* said, "The energy he has for each character is impressive and he never fails to surprise with the variety packed into the show." *Dis* was produced by WGBH TV Boston and aired on PBS affiliates across the United States. In a review of his *Us? Talking Across America*, the *Star-Phoenix* said, "His thoughtful writing combines with perfectly timed delivery to create a powerful wordscape that owes as much to jazz as drama." The *Orlando Sentinel* calls him "a modern day descendant of Woody Guthrie. He has a way with words and a wry sense of humor." He is the voice of Woody Guthrie in WCPN/National Public Radio's documentary, *Hard Travellin'*.

Recent tours have featured the author as a keynote speaker with Robert Bly at the First Coast Writer's Conference, a featured reading at City Light's Italia with Lawrence Ferlinghetti, and in performances with Yevgeny Yevtushenko on *Good Morning, Russia* and at the Moscow Polytech, the Russian Poets' Hall of Fame where he was dubbed 'The American Mayakovsky.'

CPSIA information can be obtained at www.ICGtesting.com
Printed in the USA
BVOW02s1909200813

329023BV00001B/33/A

9 781933 964140